TWO COIN

WHAT COIN?

BITCOIN

Crypto for Grownups Made as Easy as Child's Play

From *Wall Street Journal & USA Today* Bestselling Authors

Elaine Wilkes | **Dan Hollings** | **Daniel Hall**

Illustrated by *New Yorker* Magazine Cartoonist Lisa Rothstein

Published by Waterside Publishing

Buy Bitcoin, Ethereum, and crypto at your own risk!

Bitcoin and crypto don't just shoot up and never go down. It's like riding a bucking bronco in the Wild West. There can be huge ups and downs. Anything unexpected can happen with crypto, the stock market, and even the dollar.

Only invest money that you can afford to lose!

Take a moment to think about how you would feel if you lost all of your investments. If you'd feel traumatized about it, then the crypto world may not be a good fit for you. If, on the other hand, you feel comfortable with it—even a bit excited to be in on this wild ride, then let's get started.

Publisher's Cataloging-In-Publication Data
(Prepared by The Donohue Group, Inc.)

Names: Wilkes, Elaine, author. | Hollings, Dan, author. | Hall, Daniel, author. | Rothstein, Lisa (Lisa Jane), illustrator.
Title: One Coin. Two Coin. What Coin? Bitcoin: Crypto for Grownups Made as Easy as Child's Play / Elaine Wilkes, Daniel Hollings, Daniel Hall; illustrated by New Yorker Magazine cartoonist Lisa Rothstein.
Other Titles: Crypto for Grownups Made as Easy as Child's Play
Description: First edition. | [Cardiff, California]: Waterside Publishing, 2021.

Identifiers: ISBN: 978-1-954968-57-8 (paperback) |
ISBN: 978-1-954968-58-5 (ebook)
ISBN: 978-0-943941-19-6 (Audiobook)

Subjects: LCSH: Cryptocurrencies–Handbooks, manuals, etc. |
Investments–Handbooks, manuals, etc. |
Finance, Personal–Handbooks, manuals, etc.
Classification: LCC HG1710.3 .W55 2021 (print) |
LCC HG1710.3 (ebook) | DDC 332.4–dc23

BITCOIN AND CRYPTO ARE THE FUTURE

ELON MUSK

Paper money is going away.
– *Elon Musk*

Elon Musk, the founder of Tesla and SpaceX, has purchased 1.5 billion in Bitcoin.

Bitcoin has outperformed all other types of assets over the past ten years with an annualized return of over 200%. It is in a different stratosphere.
–Charlie Biello, CEO of Compound Capital Advisors

Every informed person needs to know about Bitcoin because it might be one of the world's most important developments.
– Leon Louw, two-time Nobel Peace Prize nominee

TABLE OF CONTENTS

BUT FIRST, WHY THIS BOOK?

Bitcoin? Crypto? Not sure what to do?

With this quick read, even a newbie can get in on the crypto phenomenon.

Many other crypto-made-simple books are dry, confusing, and take forever to read.

Fuhgeddaboud it—that time-sucking blah, blah, blah.

In this book, we cut to the chase and give the **FUNdamentals** in three easy steps!

1. Learn the basics.
2. Safely buy crypto.
3. Increase your earnings.

Baddabing! Baddaboom!

Numerous studies have proven that people learn better with stories, pictures, and fun.

It's best to first read Part 1—about getting into crypto. Then go back and *DO* the steps.

We take you by the mouse, and go safely...

...step-by-step, bit-by-bit, to get you started in Bitcoin and crypto.

For Part 2, we give you what we found to be the best references and info to take you further into Opportunity-Ville.

Let's do this!

NOTE:

There are no affiliate or referral commission links in this book. We make nothing, nada, zero, zip, zilch, for referring, recommending, or promoting anything besides our own fabulous "The Plan" mentioned at the end of the book.

These links are what we use and think would benefit you based on extensive use, trials, and research.

You may want to search the internet to see if you can get referral links before signing up or ordering with these other companies to get a deal.

LET'S START WITH A RHYMING WEB TIME STORY

Meet our friends, jazzy Jane and doubting Dick,

who don't know Bitcoin but need to learn quick.

Determined, as anyone watching can see,
Jane researches the new cryptocurrency.

See Dick in the corner
starting to whine,

"You don't know how to
buy Bitcoin online."

Dick huffs and puffs
while starting to yell,

"You could go broke;
you never can tell."

He snaps. "It's a bubble,
it's trouble, it'll go away."

"No," Jane states.
"After ten years,
Bitcoin is here to stay."

Here's their journey into crypto
buying that you can do too!

There's simply no denying,
this book makes it easy-to-do.

Let's sit back to see what we can learn.
The more we read, the more we can earn.

PART 1
The Basics

1
A BIT ABOUT BITCOIN AND CRYPTO

Here are the basics
for you to know,
so you can hopefully start
to make some dough.

Jane says, "I am buying crypto."

Dick asks, "What's crypto?"

MONEY VERSUS CRYPTO

Jane explains, "Dollars are paper money that you can hold and put in a physical bank.

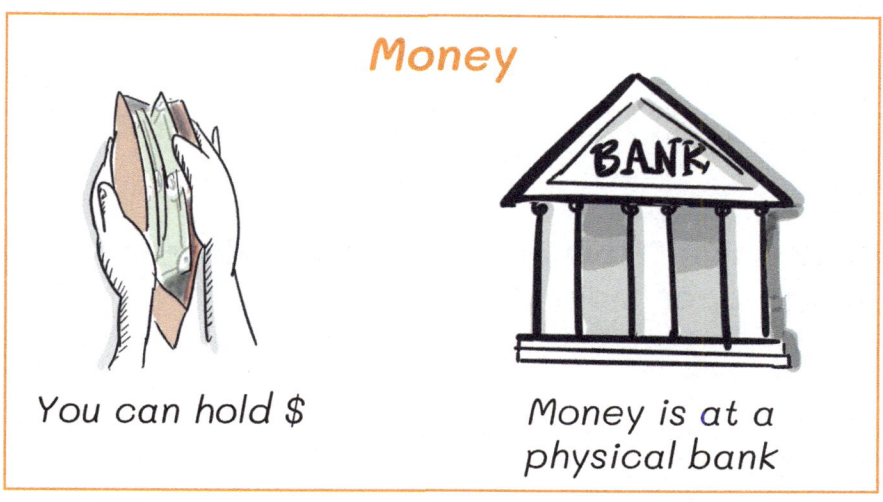

Money

You can hold $

Money is at a physical bank

Crypto, short for cryptocurrency, is digital money (coins) that you cannot hold, and it's online."

Crypto

You **cannot** hold Crypto

Crypto is ONLINE

Jane says, "There are thousands of digital coins. Bitcoin (BTC) and Ethereum (ETH) are popular examples, also known as **crypto**currencies."

CENTRALIZED VERSUS DECENTRALIZED

Dick asks, "How else is crypto different from paper money?"

Jane explains that today, your money is controlled mainly by a centralized middleman—such as a government, nation, bank, broker, or credit card company.

Centralized banking

Centralized banking has a middleman.

With cryptocurrencies, like Bitcoin and Ethereum, your finances are not under the control of any government, middleman/woman, or anyone else. It is called decentralized finance and has endless benefits.

Decentralized banking

Crypto is decentralized finance (DeFi for short) and has no middleman.

Also, you can use crypto worldwide! You simply need a cell phone (or computer) and an internet connection.

Jane: "It's secured by the blockchain."

Dick: "What's the blockchain?"

Jane: "A blockchain is a digital ledger of transactions. Each record, or block, is linked together in a list—known as a chain.

A blockchain is decentralized. It doesn't have a central point. This means that . . .
the . . . . . data . . . . .

. . . . is . . . . not . . . . .stored . . . . .
. . . . all . . . . in . . . . . . one . . . . . place.

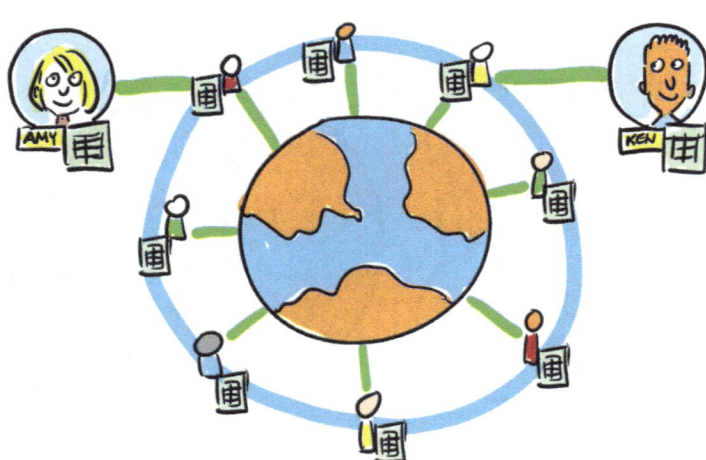

It's divided across a network of computers that act like your friends.

Let me explain: Imagine you had a dollar bill. To keep it safe, you cut it into six pieces and split it among six friends.

If someone wanted to steal your dollar bill, they would have to steal each piece from your six different friends. So it would be almost impossible.

But, if you wanted to spend your one-dollar bill, you could ask each of your six friends to give you their part, and your dollar would be whole.

Therefore, the blockchain resembles a balance sheet held in several locations until it's needed in one piece. This prevents fraud due to how hard it is to find all of the pieces."

SOME CRYPTO ADVANTAGES:

- Instant international access, 24 hours a day, seven days a week.
- Costs are much lower than at traditional banks.
- Difficult to hack.
- Vast potential of opportunities like reduced or no fees, no middleman fees, higher interest rates, and so much more.

SOME POSSIBLE CRYPTO DISADVANTAGES:

- Volatility: prices can change without warning.
- Some coins and sites are scams. The research and suggestions in this book will help you stay clear of them.

2

WHERE DO YOU BUY BITCOIN?

If you want to buy Bitcoin the right way, follow along for tips and tricks that pay!

Jane smiles. "Bitcoin and Ethereum are good coins. I'll buy those."

Dick vigorously rubs the back of his neck. "Wait! Crypto is too expensive. It costs thousands of dollars to buy Bitcoin."

You can buy just a fraction of a coin!

Jane: "I can purchase a fraction of Bitcoin for as little as $2. I'll start with buying $100 of Bitcoin."

17

Dick: "Where do you buy crypto?"

Jane: "Every person and financial situation is different. I'm researching crypto buying options."

Dick: "Why are these names crossed out on your list of places to buy crypto?"

Jane gives him the rundown of places to buy crypto:

❀ PayPal/Venmo sells only four coins: Bitcoin, Bitcoin Cash, Ethereum, and Litecoin. You don't have the freedom to move your funds or receive interest.

❀ Robinhood has your keys and doesn't allow you to transfer crypto into or out of your account. But soon you'll be able to send your coins to other wallets and receive supported crypto into your Robinhood account.

- *Square holds crypto at your own risk, and you receive zero interest. They cannot guarantee access to the platform at all times.*

- *Bitcoin vending machines and ATMs have higher fees. In one case, a 17% markup! Yikes!"*

- *Ameritrade, Schwab, Chase, Wells Fargo, and Bank of America do not sell crypto.*

- *Brokers cost too much money.*

Dick: "What about buying Bitcoin ETF's or Grayscale on the stock exchange?"

Jane: "You can't buy crypto on the stock exchanges. But there are two Bitcoin funds.

They are Grayscale Trust (Ticker: GBTC) and a ProShares Bitcoin Strategy ETF——exchange-traded fund (Ticker: BITO).

Grayscale Trust allows investors to buy shares in a trust that owns Bitcoin. The pro of owning Bitcoin in this way is it's super-duper safe. GBTC keeps its Bitcoin in a cold wallet offline and held by Coinbase.

The con to owning GBTC is there are added fees to the price of Bitcoin, known as buying at a premium. Plus, there are annual fees. Thus, it may make it more difficult to make money with GBTC as compared to owning BTC outright."

Dick: "What about the ETF? What's that?"

Jane: "Another way to invest is with the ProShares Bitcoin Strategy ETF (Ticker: BITO). This fund is pegged to Bitcoin, but it does not actually own Bitcoin—it owns futures contracts on Bitcoin. According to Investopedia: *A futures contract is a legal agreement to buy or sell a particular commodity asset, or security at a predetermined price at a specified time in the future.*"

Dick: "What the heck does that mean?"

Jane: "That like riding a roller coaster without seat belts. It can go up and down, and if you're not hanging on, you can get hurt badly.

Trading BITO can be riskier than owning Bitcoin. This is because it's based on what the future of Bicoin might be, which no one knows, and therefore, the price goes wild.

These are what's on the stock exchange. But, there are more awaiting approval and may be available soon."

Dick scratches his head. "How do you know the best place to buy crypto?"

Jane: "One way is to use a crypto exchange or savings platform to turn your money into crypto. Like when you go to Europe, you exchange your US dollars for Euros. It's the same thing; only instead of Euros, you're changing your money for digital crypto coins. It's also like buying stocks at a stock exchange, only you buy crypto (like Bitcoin and Ethereum) at a crypto exchange or crypto bank called a savings platform."

Jane: "You need a crypto exchange or savings platform (like a bank account) that is:

1. Super-duper safe and secure
2. Easy for beginners to use
3. Offers flexibility, so you can do many things with the coins
4. Trusted

"Oh look! Coinbase, Gemini, and Nexo fit all four requirements. We'll use those for now to get started."

NOTE—IF YOU'RE OUTSIDE THE U.S.
Most non-U.S citizens (depending on the country) can buy crypto directly at Nexo.io (a savings platform) and earn up to 12% interest there. If you want to trade crypto, then consider these exchanges: KuCoin.com, Binance.com, or FTX.com.

Jane: "If you **ONLY want to save crypto** and earn high interest while the coin goes up or down in value, then save at crypto banks like Gemini and/or Nexo.io. I'll start buying and saving crypto at Gemini.com because it's one of the easiest platforms to use, and I don't have to move crypto or wire money to another place to save it.

Nexo.io has way better interest rates than Gemini. Most non-U.S. residents can buy directly on Nexo. But U.S. and Australian residents must transfer crypto or wire money into Nexo, which is not as easy as buying at Gemini and Coinbase. So first, I'll get my toes wet with Gemini, which is the easiest. Later, when I know more, I can then try wiring and transferring funds.

For security, Coinbase, Gemini, and many other crypto companies have **KYC—K**now **Y**our **C**ustomer. That means when I sign up, I need to upload (digitally send) my driver's license, I.D. card, or passport to prove who I am."

Dick: "Wait! You'll be giving out all your info! Can you trust them? You could get scammed or have identity theft!"

Jane: "Don't worry. Coinbase and Gemini are like the PayPal of Crypto. They're ultra-secure, legit, and trusted cryptocurrency exchanges on the internet. I'll also take safety precautions."

PROTECT YOUR CRYPTO BY USING THESE SECURITY TIPS:

- Use a private, encrypted email address from Proton (https://protonmail.com) that you use only for crypto—nothing else. Do not give this email address to anyone.

- For every site where you sign up, use a password that's strong, long (at least 12 characters), and that you've never used before.

- Sites starting with https://.... are much more secure than http://—without the "s."

- Do not use words, names, birthdates, hometowns, or an easy-to-figure-out password. Use uppercase and lowercase characters.

- You can take a long sentence you'll remember and use the first letter of each word! Yctalsyrautfloew! would be the password for the last sentence.

- Do not store passwords on your computer or cell phone. Instead, write your passwords on paper or in the journal at the end of this book. Or use http://LastPass.com.

- Store the papers safely in a fireproof box and keep another copy, or this book, in a different, secure location as a backup.

- Keep track of everything on paper. Write down your logins and passwords for every crypto site. In some cases, if you lose your login details, you can lose your crypto. There also may be no technical support or help. So from day one, **KEEP TRACK OF YOUR PASSWORDS AND LOGINS!**

8 Put all logins in your will and mention who will inherit your crypto. Otherwise, it can be bye-bye to all of your crypto if no one knows your logins, where your crypto is, or even that you own it.

SUPER-DUPER IMPORTANT SAFETY TIP!

NEVER click on an email or text link from a crypto company. Instead, type in their domain name in your browser and access their site that way—**NOT BY A LINK!**

> Text Message
> Today 10:52 AM
>
> To celebrate the release of the new Celsius Web App, HODL your crypto with the Web App and receive up to $2,000 in bonus: https:// celsius.loan/

Text from Scammer

The identical, fake site from the text is Celsius. loan—not Celsius. network (the real Celsius site). So a friend lost $28,000 because he gave the scammer his info, thinking it was Celsius.

Do not give anyone your crypto info.

Scammers also do this with non-crypto sites.

Jane: "Now let's find out more about crypto banks and discover how their interest rates are way up, up, up compared to traditional banks."

3
CRYPTO HIGH-INTEREST SAVINGS ACCOUNTS

**Traditional bank interest rates
are way too low.
With crypto's high-interest rates,
you can watch your money grow.**

Jane: "I'm researching the **new** crypto banking."

Dick: "What's that?"

Jane: "At the moment, I have my savings in a traditional bank where they charge lots of fees and pay me meager crumbs of interest.

  Instead, I'll hodl, which means hold or save, some of my crypto in crypto banks that have no transfer and withdrawal fees, along with having higher interest rates."

FUN FACT:
Hodl means hold, but because of someone's typo, the word hodl stuck!

Dick: "Can you hold, or as you say, hodl, your crypto at Coinbase?"

Jane: "No, Coinbase doesn't offer high-interest savings. However, an online crypto bank offers high-interest savings.

After all my research, I'll start with Gemini.com because it's one of the easiest to use. It's for newbies and is available in all U.S. states and various countries. The rates change often. Now I can earn 1.49% for Bitcoin and up to 8.05% interest on their stablecoins, which we'll discuss later. There are no minimum requirements or penalties for withdrawing." "

Dick: "Whoa! Wait a minute! Are you sure this interest is legit? Maybe it's a scam!"

Jane: "Gemini has industry-leading, world-class security. They're the world's first crypto exchange to complete exams conducted by Deloitte & Touche LLC, showing they have the security and compliance levels to benefit the customer. They also have high insurance coverage and use the best-in-industry cold storage coverage."

> Gemini is well-funded, reliable, highly secure, and one of the most reputable exchanges in the world.

Vote 2019 Markets Choice Awards "Best Crypto Exchange"

The world's first SOC 1 Type 1 and SOC 2 Type 1 and 2 certified crypto exchange and custodian.

Dick: "I'll keep my U.S. dollars in a traditional U.S. bank's savings account like I've always done."

See Dick earn .02% interest on his U.S. savings account.

See his nest egg's interest go

down

down

down.

Jane: "Let's compare the difference in interest between Gemini's savings and a traditional bank savings account. I'm using a coin called a stablecoin since, like the dollar, it will not fluctuate in price.

It stays pretty much the same value. So after ten years, here are the differences."

Both are starting with $10,000. At the end of ten years, the interest =	
Gemini Crypto Bank (For a stablecoin with an interest rate of 8.05% APY)	**Traditional U.S. Bank** Compounded monthly (Saving interest at 0.02% APY)
Interest earned = $11,689.41	**Interest earned = $20.02**

Dick: "Yeah, but this tech crypto stuff is confusing."

Jane: "Gemini's site has beginner options that are clutter-free and simple to use. Signing up is easy and takes only minutes."

> **Text Message**
> Today 7:04 PM
>
> Coinbase: We have received a withdrawal request from an unknown device. If this was not you, follow the steps here: https://restore31651-coinbase-us.web.app

ANOTHER SCAM— DON'T CLICK THE LINK!

FYI. If you start trading crypto, upgrade to Gemini's free ActiveTraderTM account. But, for U.S. lower fees, check out Kraken.com, Binance.us, or Gate.io. For non-U.S, see KuCoin.com, Binance.com, or FTX.com.

Dick: "So do you buy crypto from Gemini, then put it in their high-interest savings?"

Jane: "You don't have to know how to move crypto to other places. At Gemini, everything is all under one roof. You can save it while it earns interest, buy it, or sell it. In addition, Gemini is coming out with a Bitcoin credit card."

Dick: "Bitcoin credit card! Does that mean I make purchases with Bitcoin?"

Jane: "Nope. Gemini partnered with Mastercard, so it's just like using a regular credit card.

Only with Gemini's credit card, instead of cash-back rewards, they give you 3% crypto-back rewards.

The card will pay rewards in more than 30 cryptocurrencies. You choose the crypto you want for your rewards."

Dick: "How do you sign up for a Gemini account?"

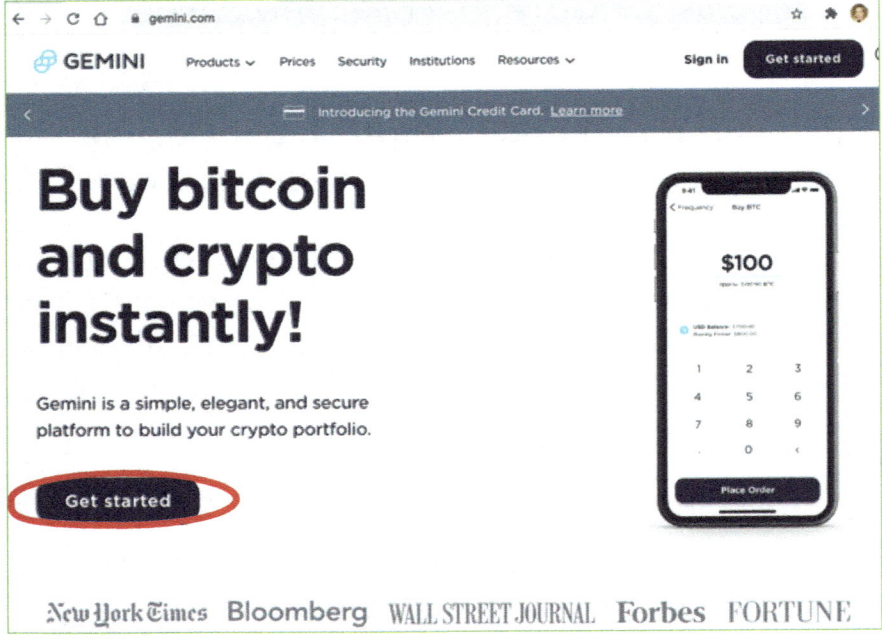

Jane: "It takes minutes to open a Gemini account. Go to Gemini.com. Click on the **Get Started** button. Fill out your info. Then, Gemini requires 2-Factor Authentication, also called 2FA."

Dick: "What's 2FA?"

Jane: "2-Factor Authentication is an additional security method for your account. You can use it to secure your favorite sites too. If your password gets stolen, the thief can't access your account without the second step. It works like this:

1. Use your password to log into an account.

2. The 2FA adds a second method of identity by sending a time-sensitive code to your phone or computer app to verify it's you. This protects your accounts since the scammer would need both your computer and cell phone.

*2FA helps
protect your accounts.*

Get the free 2FA app at: https://authy.com

Jane: "Then after you're verified, click the **Add Funding Source** button. Choose **Automatically Link Bank Account**—any choice there is fine. It uses Plaid, so it's secure. After you add your bank account, it shows up under **Linked Funding Sources.**

Then on the main page, it says to confirm your email. So go into your email and confirm it.

Then, it's easy to add your ID by following simple instructions. That was a breeze!

Now that I have a crypto account, I'm going to buy Bitcoin."

4
BUY CRYPTO TO EARN HIGH INTEREST

If you want to hold crypto
for a long while,
get high-interest rates
that'll make you smile.

Jane: "I'm excited to buy crypto since on Gemini, I can earn interest on up to 30 different types of coins, including Bitcoin and Ethereum. I can withdraw anytime without penalties."

Here's their crypto calculator to figure out how much you'll earn on each coin. (stablecoins are mentioned later.)
https://www.gemini.com/earn

Dick: "Does Gemini have the best interest rates?"

Jane: "Nexo.io and other savings platforms have much higher interest rates. Many non-U.S. residents can buy directly from Nexo. But U.S. and Australian citizens can't buy directly on Nexo (unless it's over 60K). They can wire money in, or the coins have to be purchased from a crypto exchange like Coinbase, then transferred into Nexo. When I know how to do that, I'll save at Nexo too. It's good to diversify."

Dick: "How do you buy Bitcoin?"

Jane: "I log into Gemini. com. I click on Bitcoin. Then click Buy and follow the prompts. Next, I can click one-time order. (Or, later on, I can schedule deposits.) I then put in the amount I want to buy and click the "Place Order" button. It shows "Success!" That's it. It's so easy-peasy lemon breezy, which is why I'm first buying crypto at Gemini."

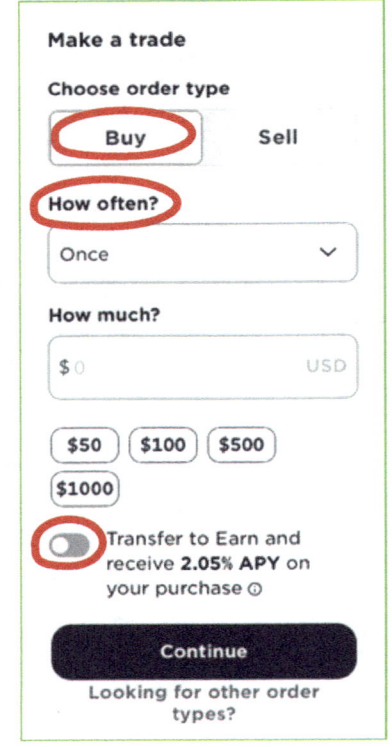

With this account, I can also set up autopay for DCA (Dollar- Cost

Averaging) for a recurring buy with a specific smaller amount of money to invest over a set amount of time, rather than buying one lump sum. DCA is a strategy of Warren Buffet."

Dollar-cost averaging (DCA) calculator for Bitcoin: https://dcabtc.com

Jane: "I did it! I own Bitcoin. Yay!"

Jane researches more on the internet the pros and cons of crypto dollar-cost averaging to find out if it's right for her.

Jane writes down her logins, passwords, and the amount she spent in her crypto journal (in the back of this book).

Jane: "Next, I'll sign up with Coinbase. I can do more with my coins there. This is fun!"

5
USING THE
COINBASE EXCHANGE

**To do more with your crypto,
let's learn about Coinbase.
There you can trade, sell,
and move coins to another place.**

Jane explains that Coinbase is another exchange that is easy to use for buying and selling crypto.

Coinbase is a popular and well-known crypto exchange. It:

- has over 30 million users.
- has traded over $150 billion.
- is supported in 100 countries.
- is backed by trusted investors.
- has an IPO on the stock exchange.
- had one of the most successful IPO's in U.S. history.

You can use Coinbase to start trading and also to move coins to save at crypto banks like Nexo.

Of course, if you ONLY want to hodl your coins at Gemini, you don't need to sign up at Coinbase.

Jane: "I'm ready to sign up at Coinbase by clicking this link: https://www.coinbase.com/signup

Click this link for step-by-step instructions on how to sign up with Coinbase: https://bit.ly/3xFRlqN

(For lower fees, non-U.S. citizens can use other exchanges like Binance, KuCoin, or FTX.)

The third step has several ways to get your driver's license (or another identity document) to Coinbase. Choose the one that works best for you:

Taking pictures of your ID:

- Use your computer's camera or phone to take a picture of the front and back of your driver's license or ID.

Uploading ID pictures:

- ☙ If you used your cell phone, transfer the pictures by sending them from your phone to your computer photo gallery, which most phones do automatically. You can also email them from your phone to your computer. Then you can send them to Coinbase.

- ☙ Or, download Coinbase's mobile app onto your cellphone and sign in. Then just upload the pictures from your phone.

The last set-up step for Coinbase:

Jane links her bank account as her payment method to buy crypto. In some cases, there may be a waiting period of 1-10 days for funds to clear with a free ACH bank transfer. Wire transfers are $10 inbound and $25 outbound, but the funds are available quickly. Paying with PayPal has a 2.5% fee.

Coinbase fees: https://bit.ly/3qgbGRO
Linking your payment method to Coinbase

Here's how to link your payment method:
https://bit.ly/3gKdIpl

Here's info on adding your bank account:
https://bit.ly/2UfAxbA

Basically, when you're logged into Coinbase.com, select the last icon on the right (the one with your name on it). Next, use the pull-down menu to select **Settings,** then **Payment Methods.**

Select **Add a Payment Method.** Select the type of account you want.

Follow the instructions for complete verification, which will differ depending on the type of account being linked.

Jane: "I am buying $100 of Bitcoin at Coinbase."

Here's how to buy crypto on Coinbase:
https://bit.ly/35GcJjF

Jane logs into her Coinbase account. She clicks the **Buy/Sell** button on the right side of the screen.

This window pops up.

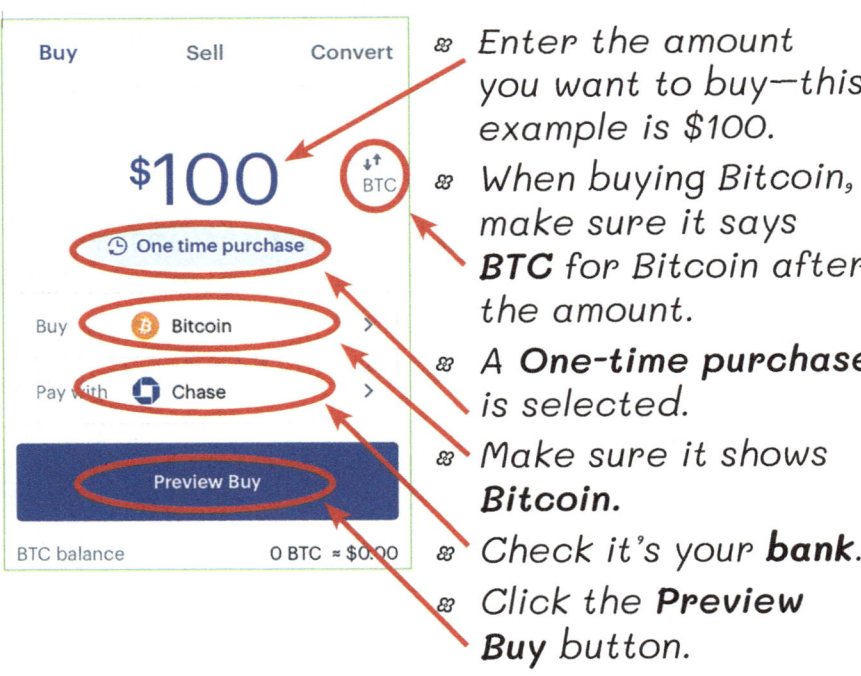

- Enter the amount you want to buy—this example is $100.
- When buying Bitcoin, make sure it says **BTC** for Bitcoin after the amount.
- A **One-time purchase** is selected.
- Make sure it shows **Bitcoin.**
- Check it's your **bank**.
- Click the **Preview Buy** button.

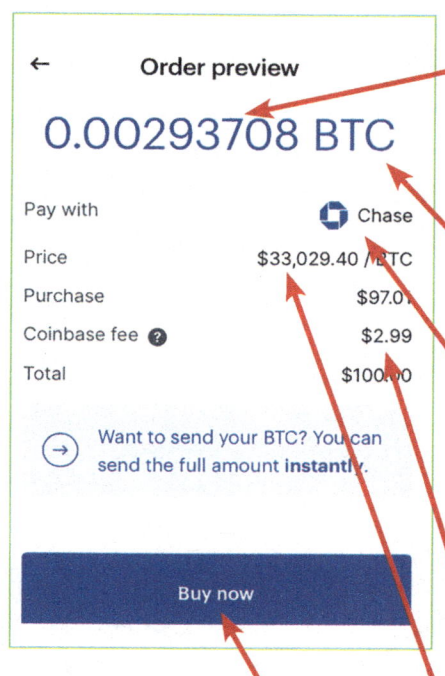

Order preview

0.00293708 BTC

Pay with	◆ Chase
Price	$33,029.40 /BTC
Purchase	$97.01
Coinbase fee ❓	$2.99
Total	$100.00

→ Want to send your BTC? You can send the full amount **instantly**.

Buy now

☙ BTC's long number is in Bitcoin currency, not dollars. That's how much Bitcoin you'll have.

☙ Make sure it shows the coin you are buying.

☙ Pay with your bank account, not a credit card that has higher fees. Do not borrow to buy crypto!

☙ In this case, Coinbase takes a $2.99 fee.

☙ The $33,029.40 BTC price is the current Bitcoin price, NOT how much you're buying.

☙ Click the **Buy now** button. Out of the $100 invested, you own $97.01 of Bitcoin.

Whoopee, Jane just bought Bitcoin!

She scribbles down the sale in her crypto journal at the back of this book. She then looks into buying Ethereum while considering her crypto budget.

Jane and her dog, Doge, do their happy dance.

6
SEE JANE BUY ETHEREUM

The crypto market is open around the clock, so you can buy crypto any time, unlike stock.

Late one night, Jane and Dick look at other crypto coins. Unlike the stock market, crypto exchanges are open 24/7. Jane can buy any amount at any time.

Jane: "I will now buy $100 of Ethereum. It's a top-rated coin that's predicted to go up, up, up."

Dick: **"But that goes up and down, and up, and down. You could lose your money!"**

Jane: "Ethereum is forecasted to increase over time, so I'll take my chances. Could you be fear-casting?"

*Here's an example of how to buy $100 of Ethereum on Coinbase. (Of course, **if you ONLY want to hodl it and have an account with Gemini, you can buy Ethereum directly from Gemini.**) Do the same as before, except you'll need to select Ethereum instead of Bitcoin.*

Log into your Coinbase account.
Click the blue **Buy/Sell** *button.*

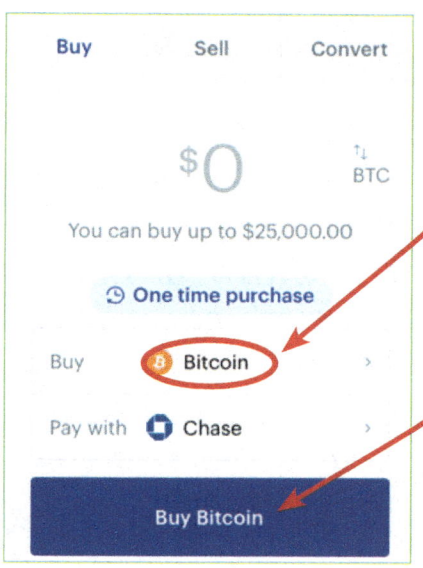

How to buy Ethereum instead of Bitcoin.

- ✍ *This time click on the orange **Bitcoin** button to change it to Ethereum.*

- ✍ *When you click on the **Buy/Sell** button list of other coins will come up.*

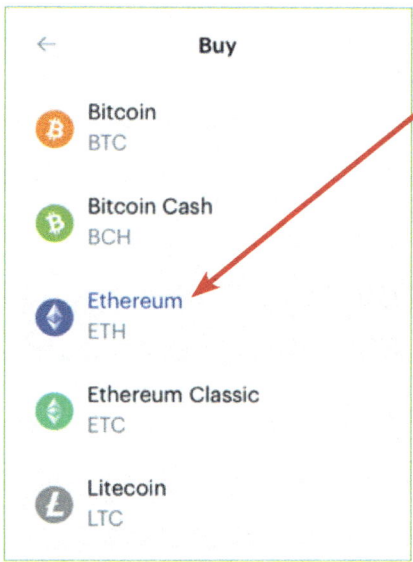

- ✍ *Click on **Ethereum (ETH).** That changes BTC to ETH on the next screen.*
*The **Buy** tab now shows **ETH** (Ethereum) instead of Bitcoin.*

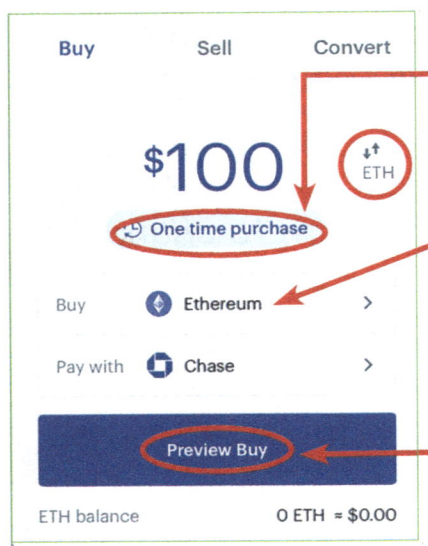

- Make sure **One time purchase** is selected.
- Make sure you see **Ethereum (ETH).** Pay with your bank account, not a credit card.
- Click **Preview Buy.** Your order preview will come up.

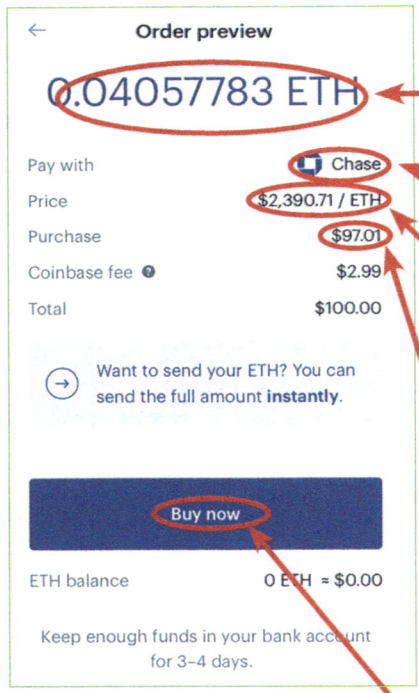

- The top number is the amount of Ethereum you're buying.
- Pay with your bank account.
- The $2390.71 is Ethereum's current market price, NOT how much you are buying.
- $97.01 is the amount of ETH you own after Coinbase's fee is deducted.
- You've invested a total of $100.
- Click the **Buy now** button.

Here's the same example, but this time we're investing $1,000 of Ethereum **(ETH)** to show the difference in fees as you invest more money.

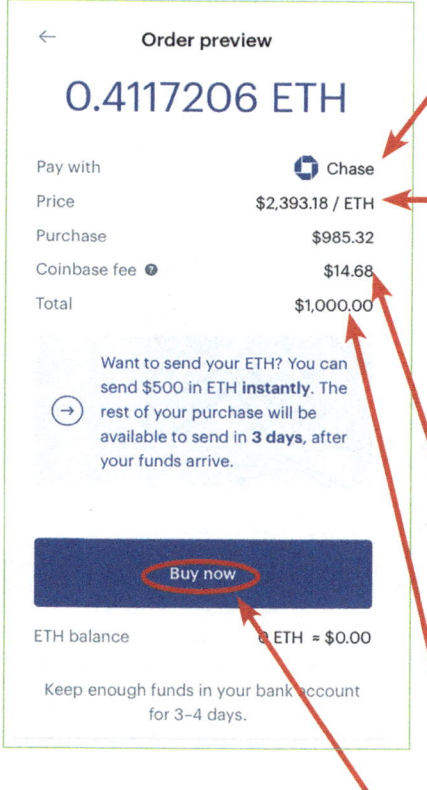

☙ Pay with your bank, not your credit card.

☙ *Make sure it says* **ETH** *for Ethereum since that's what you're buying.*

☙ Ethereum's market value is $2,393.18, NOT how much you're buying.

☙ *Coinbase takes a percentage of the transaction. This time it's a* **$14.68** *fee.*

☙ Total owned is $985.32 of ETH from a $1,000 order.

☙ Click the **Buy now** button.

Jane now owns fractions of both Bitcoin and Ethereum!

She feels confident and proud of herself for learning to buy crypto and is excited to see the progress of her investments.

Next, she'll learn how to move coins to other places.

7
HOW TO TRANSFER YOUR COINS ELSEWHERE

Here's how to transfer coins out of Coinbase, so you can use your coins at another place.

Jane: "Now, in just a few clicks, I can move my coins from Coinbase to places like Nexo, other exchanges, and more. Here's how I transfer coins from one place to another. In this example, I'll transfer my crypto from Coinbase to Nexo."

Dick: "Be careful because if you do something wrong, you can lose your money forever! Say bye-bye to your coins. You need to give this all your attention."

Jane: "It's important to follow the instructions carefully https://bit.ly/3cZoISO and do a test with a small bit of money to make sure I transfer it correctly.

Once I do the test, I'll get verification that it was sent and received. Then I'll transfer the other crypto. Transferring crypto from one place to another is pretty much the same procedure everywhere."

Dick: "Be careful. If one number or letter is off, you could lose your money."

Jane: "I just transferred a small amount as a test.

Yay, the email says it was delivered to Nexo, and my Bitcoin is at Nexo! So now I'll send more crypto since I did it correctly."

WHEN TRANSFERRING CRYPTO— ALWAYS TEST FIRST!!!

If you do something wrong, you can lose your crypto forever. First, conduct a test by transferring a small amount of money first before you send everything.

WIRE MONEY INTO NEXO

Residents outside the U.S. can buy direct on Nexo. U.S. and Australian residents need to wire money into Nexo first, then swap it for crypto. Here's a step-by-step article on how to do that so you can earn super-duper high interest. https://bit.ly/3OGDzsx

To stay organized, Jane keeps track in her crypto journal. See the back of this book.

She also adds her logins and passwords to her will.

Dick: "When do you earn interest?"

Jane: "I automatically earn high interest right away—hooray! I can earn higher interest at other places, but Gemini is easier. If you're comfortable using the computer, you may want to use savings platforms like Nexo that pay higher interest. There can be more steps involved. But for newbies, Gemini is one of the easiest to use."

8
DIPPITY DOO–DAH, DIPPITY DAYS

And with the flick of a wick
on a bright red candlestick,
even though Bitcoin took a dive,
Jane thought her account would soon thrive.

Dick: "There's a huge dip! Bitcoin and Ethereum are down,

down,

down.

You're losing money! Sell!"

Jane: "That's A-OK. I'm in it for the long term."

Dick: "Stop. Get out. You're losing money!"

Jane: "Crypto prices go up and down and up—like a roller coaster."

Dick: "But you're

LOSING MONEY!"

Jane: "I sometimes buy on the dips. It's like a sale. And when it turns around and is high, with some coins, I can also take a little profit along the way."

Days later . . .

Dick: "WHOA! Everything is up so high. Maybe we should buy more now."

Jane: "Welcome to the crypto roller coaster ride. Let's not get emotional with FOMO (**F**ear **O**f **M**issing **O**ut). We need a solid plan.

Maybe we can put in a certain amount every month, like **D**ollar **C**ost **A**veraging (**DCA**), or I call it, **D**igital **C**oin **A**veraging?

Let's decide what percentage of our savings we want to invest in crypto.

Maybe we take some profits along the way. But we need to talk to an accountant or tax professional about crypto capital gains taxes.

We could also hold some for a long-term investment and not worry about the ups and downs. Let's research this and figure out what's best for us to create a strategy."

Dick: "That's a good idea."

9
STORING CRYPTO?

**You can also keep your crypto
off the internet,
only if you have a safe password
you don't forget.**

Dick: "What are crypto wallets?"

Jane: "The crypto I buy is stored in a wallet. Think of how you keep your physical money in a wallet. But the crypto wallet has a key that goes with it. Instead of a physical key, it's a string of numbers. However, if I buy crypto at an exchange, they hold my keys. So that's why it's not a good idea to store your money on an exchange."

Dick: "I hear about a hot wallet and a cold wallet for storing crypto. What's that?"

HOT WALLET

COLD WALLET

Jane: "A hot wallet is when you store crypto online or on your computer. You do have a small risk of being hacked.

A cold wallet is when you store it offline, so it has no chance of being hacked online. It can be an external drive or look like a thumb drive, but it holds crypto offline. That means your private keys are not connected to the internet. Only the owner has access to the crypto.

But if the owner forgets or loses the passwords, then he or she can lose all their crypto."

Dick: "A guy purchased Bitcoin ten years ago. He stored it on an external device with a strong password.

Now it's worth over $200 million.

BUT . . . he forgot the password! Shucks!

He has no idea what the password is.

He has two more tries, and if he doesn't get it right, the drive is wiped out, and he'll lose all $200+ million."

See the full story here: https://bit.ly/3gLO5UY
and here: https://nyti.ms/3gOlxcy

59

Jane: "That guy had a cold wallet that had only ten password guesses. But these days, cold wallets have recovery passcodes. So, if you've lost your password, you can use all these passcodes to recover your crypto. But it's still imperative to keep all your passwords safe."

Tresor and Ledger offer cold wallets starting at $60. Hot wallets like Exodus, Metamask, and Coinbase are some online choices.

In summary, think of this analogy. Hot wallets are like going to the bank's teller. Cold wallets are like going to the bank's vault.

The advantage of having a cold wallet is you are 100% in control of your crypto. You're not vulnerable to any shutdowns or anything else happening externally. "Not your keys, not your crypto" is a popular saying. With cold storage, you have your keys. You also can't get hacked unless someone takes your device.

The disadvantage is there's no support. If you lose your login, password, or device, you can lose your crypto. Also, it does not earn interest. But staking is a way to earn rewards/passive income on certain crypto that you hold in a cold wallet from Ledger. These are called "Staking Pools" and are like bank savings accounts. The reason your crypto earns rewards while staked is because the blockchain puts it to work while it's held in your cold wallet.

Jane and Dick decide to keep their crypto at crypto savings banks (like Gemini and Nexo) to diversify platforms and earn high interest.

Jane learns about trading and storing her crypto in a crypto IRA that makes her earnings in that account tax-sheltered.

TIPS ON HARDWARE (COLD-OFFLINE) WALLETS:

- If you forget your passwords, you can lose your crypto. So always store the key phrases in a fireproof box for safekeeping. Also, keep a backup of the phrases in another safe place.

- Never have someone set this up for you. If anyone else has your key phrases, they can access your wallet and steal all your money.

- Do not store phrases on your cell phone, computer, or the internet. These places can be hacked.

- Do NOT buy a cold wallet from eBay or any second-party seller. Make sure you are buying your drive directly from the company that makes it. If you purchase it from a second-party seller, it's possible that they programed your drive in a way that allows them to steal your money. Make sure the box your drive arrives in has never been opened.

10
CRYPTO IRAs

**Start saving for your future retirement
in a new tax-sheltered way,
with a crypto trading and savings account
owned by your IRA.**

Jane: "It's great I'm making so much money in crypto. But with every trade, I get taxed—that's not great.

And if I make a ton of money, I'll get taxed on that too.

However, if I get a crypto **IRA**—**I**ndividual **R**etirement **A**ccount, I get unlimited tax-sheltered trades. Depending on the IRA, I can get deferred or tax-sheltered earnings."

Dick: "A CRYPTO IRA! How does that work?"

Jane: "Of all my assets, I think I'll earn the most with my crypto. But I must pay taxes on them. Ouch! That could be A LOT of money I'd have to pay Uncle Sam.

But, depending on the IRA, I could take that same money and put it into a crypto Roth IRA. Then, when I retire and sell my crypto, I could pay zero taxes on hopefully huge profits.

Awesome sauce!

Roth IRAs are one of the best ways to grow wealth. Being in the U.S., we should ALWAYS max out our Roths. The money is taxed going in but not coming out. That means it could grow like wildfire, and I'm not burned by taxes. I'm not taxed on all those gains."

> **NOTE:**
> *Cointracking.info software keeps track of your crypto taxes for non-IRA accounts.*

Dick: "Yeah, but what could go wrong with a crypto IRA?"

Jane: "Crypto is volatile, so you can gain or lose your money. There can be large rewards and great risks too. It can be very risky for some people, especially if that's all they have."

Dick: "How's a crypto IRA different from a brokerage IRA?"

Jane: "They both offer all types of IRAs, like Roth and Traditional IRAs. The difference is one uses money, and the other can use crypto. They both have penalties if I withdraw early.

The brokerage is FDIC insured. We need to make sure to use a crypto exchange that's insured and secure. Luckily, I've found some companies that offer this."

Dick: "How much can you put into a crypto IRA?"

Jane: "For example, with a Roth IRA, it says here that you can only use earned, taxed income. If you're under 50 years old, the most you can put in is $6,000, and from age 50, you can put in up to $7,000.

You can also move all or part of the money from an entire traditional IRA into a crypto account."

Dick: "Can we create a crypto IRA at a brokerage?"

Jane: "Brokerages don't deal in crypto. Instead, we hire a company to set up a crypto IRA account for us, which is easy to do and takes minutes."

Dick: "What are the rules?"

Jane: "Unlike a traditional IRA that doesn't have income restrictions, you're not eligible for a Roth IRA if you're single and earn over $139,000 a year or a married couple filing jointly who earn over $206,000 a year. If someone makes more than that, they may want to check out the Backdoor ROTH IRA."

Dick: "How do we get started?"

Jane: "We can move a current IRA to a crypto IRA, which is a tax-sheltered incident. Also, in minutes, a company (like the ones below) will set up a new crypto IRA account for tax-shielded trading and high-interest savings."

CRYPTO IRA COMPANIES:

www.broadfinancial.com

www.IRAfinancial.com

CRYPTO PENSION AND PROFITS SHARING PLANS:

www.VastSolutionsGroup.com

Dick and Jane are surprised at how fast and easy it was to set up. They feel great knowing they're helping their future selves.

Jane proceeds to learn about earning super high savings interest rates with stablecoins.

11
GET HIGH INTEREST ON U.S. DOLLARS

I turn my dollars into
stablecoins now,
so I earn super high interest—
I'll show you how.

Jane: "Stablecoins earn 12% interest at Nexo and 8.05% interest at Gemini (rates will vary). They don't have wild price fluctuations and stay at $1.00 or close to it."

Dick: "What's a stablecoin?"

Jane: "Stablecoins are backed by the U.S. dollar. Since they're basically worth one dollar, they don't have huge up-and-down swings in price. Stablecoins are designed to minimize price volatility. That's why they're called **stable**coins.

At Nexo, stablecoins, USDC (USD Coin), USDT (Tether), and DAI earn 12% interest. Those coins aim to keep their value as close to one United States dollar as possible.

Gemini pays (rates will vary) 8.05% for DAI and for its own Gemini stablecoin (GUSD), which is always convertible to exactly $1 at Gemini."

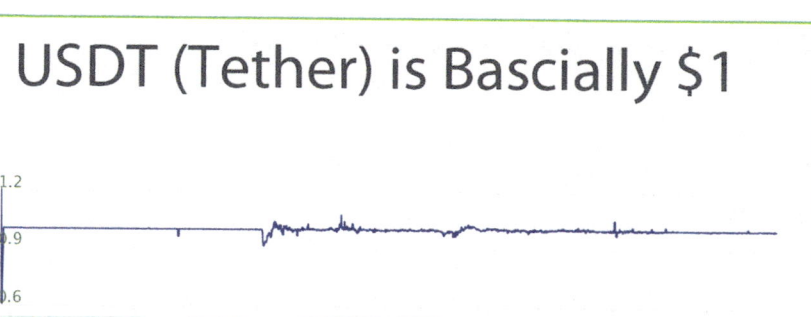

A STABLECOIN CHART
VS.
BITCOIN'S NON-STABLECOIN CHART

Dick: "How do I buy stablecoins?"

Jane: "You can buy stablecoins on just about every exchange and transfer wherever you want it."

This video explains a Nexo savings account: https://bit.ly/3gTCRg2

Research to find what option is best for you. We've mentioned this to show there are US stablecoins that can earn very high interest daily. They are not volatile. You can withdraw your money anytime, and there are no fees. The various stablecoins earn different interest rates—up to 12%.

12
CASHING OUT YOUR COINS

**You may want to sell
some coins along the way,
so with your profit,
you can go out and play.**

Dick and Jane decide to sell some of their coins at a profit, very similar to how investors take profits with stock gains.

Dick: "We've made money. How can we sell our crypto and convert it into paper money that we can actually spend?"

Jane: "It's easy. It's just like how we sent money to the exchange when buying crypto, but instead, when selling, we're sending it from the exchange to our bank.

To sell our crypto, we put a sell order in instead of a buy order.

We click the Buy/Sell button at the top of the page on Coinbase.

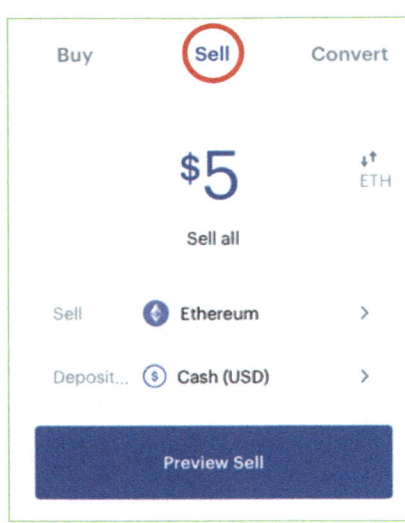

Then, it's the same process we did buying crypto, only instead of clicking **Buy**, we click **Sell** and enter what we want to sell and how much.

And voila! We have our money."

Dick: "I checked the bank, and our profit is there."

Most exchanges have the same setup to take profits along the way.

Dick sees the light after comparing their crypto profits to the stock market and their bank interest. Then, Dick joins Jane in learning more about buying and selling crypto. They look over their finances, develop a crypto plan, and don't emotionally buy or sell on impulse.

They go over their budget and decide how much they want to put into crypto.

They do a lot of research on crypto coins. Some coins they hodl, but other coins, when the coin is up, they sell and take their profit.

Strategies vary for each person but make sure you think of a strategy.

Together, Jane and Dick learn more and more as time passes on.

13
ONE YEAR LATER

Dick and Jane put the majority
of their crypto away.
Because they saved a lot of money,
now they can travel and play.

As Dick and Jane lay out in the warm sun on
an exotic island, they reflect on their crypto
journey.

Dick: "Since you taught me what to do, I bought the coins and watched them grow. I made all this money from making wise purchases. It's amazing how I made money while I slept and did other things."

"Oh my, this is fun!" laughs Jane. "It paid off learning to invest and hodl crypto."

Dick: "Yeah, but most of all, I love hodling you!"

Jane and Dick are traveling the world, happy as can be.

They don't have to work at jobs because they're rich.

Jane and Dick live happily ever after.

THE END???

The above ending could happen, but another
outcome could be that they lose their money.
Investing is risky. Here are some money tips,
so your story has a great chance at
happily ever after.

Be wise, be prudent,
and be cautious as well.
Be filled with knowledge
before you buy or sell.

14
HOW TO LOSE MONEY IN CRYPTO

- **FREAK OUT! Sell because of a market dip.**

    When you're freaking out, that's when the smart money is buying. A dip means that it went down, but it usually doesn't stay down forever. For example, if you look at Bitcoin's  history, it goes down and up a lot. Get ready for the roller coaster ride.

- **Fall for scams, get rich quick crypto and take "hot tips" from anyone.**

- **Borrowing to buy crypto.**

    Borrowing or putting crypto purchases on a credit card is a definite NO! Don't do it.

⚅ Make decisions out of fear.

If you're constantly afraid of losing your money, guess what will happen?

⚅ Human errors.

Transferring your crypto to the wrong address, losing passwords, giving out your wallet info, and so on.

MORAL OF THE STORY:

1. Be mindful AND READY FOR VOLATILITY.

2. Slow down.

3. Double-check everything you do in crypto.

4. Know what you're doing. Learn Crypto.

15
SUCCESS TIPS FOR CRYPTO LAND

- Only invest what you can afford to lose.

- **BEFORE** investing, consult with a licensed financial professional or accountant to make sure it's right for you, and your financial circumstances.

- Building a better financial future requires skill, sound financial management, and a calm, unemotional approach.

- **Test** any new investment with **small** amounts of your savings.

- Keep your initial investments small. Example: If you have $100,000 in savings, don't risk more than $2,000 to $5,000.

- Figure out and use a percent of your savings as a rule. Example: Don't risk more than 2-5% of your savings on any investment.

- Save to Invest. Save as much as you can of your monthly take-home pay.
  Example: If you earn $100,000 a year, you should save at least 20%.

- Open every tax shielded account you can—non-crypto and crypto IRAs and 401(k)s. This can save you A LOT of money.

- Invest wisely in your IRAs. Consider putting a set percentage of your retirement account savings into an indexed broad equity ETF or mutual fund such as SPDR Dow Jones Industrial Average (DIA).

- Optimize your workplace 401k and take advantage of any matching.

- Taxes: Because gains and losses can be so significant with crypto, smart money always considers the effect of taxes. Look into short and long-term capital gains.

- Diversify and create an achievable plan.

Dick and Jane took control of their finances, spilled over into helping other areas of their lives.

You have the steps here. Choose what's best for you.

PART 2
Going Further with Crypto

YOUR NEXT STEPS . . .

Your adventure into Cryptoland
has only just begun.

There's so much more to see and do.
It's exponentially fun!

Turn one coin into two coins,
into three coins before your eyes.

You'll grin and smile from ear to ear
as you grow your ROIs.

Where's the secret path? You ask,
oh please, a helping hand?

You're almost there!

Your next step . . .

You're invited to
"The Plan."
Go here:
www.ThePlanRocks.com

CRYPTO RESOURCES YOU'LL WANNA KNOW

Here's the stuff we're using that we think could possibly benefit you too.

There are no affiliate or referral commission links in this book. We make nothing, nada, zero, zip, zilch, for referring, recommending, or promoting anything besides our own fabulous "The Plan" see www.ThePlanRocks.com.

Some links were shortened because they were too long. They are not affiliate links. The links are based on extensive use, trials, and research. Therefore, you may want to search the internet to see if you can get referral links before signing up or ordering from these other companies to get a deal.

NEXO LOANS

Nexo is also a top-rated, extremely low- interest loan crypto bank.
https://www.Nexo.io

CRYPTO TRADING PLATFORMS TO CONSIDER

For U.S.:
Kraken.com
Binance.US

For Non-U.S.:
Binance.com
Kucoin.com
FTX.com

CRYPTO CALCULATOR AND CONVERTER

This crypto calculator figures out what a coin is worth, then calculates it from US dollars to another coin or vice versa.
https://bit.ly/3xE1jZQ

HOT TIP:
Siri (iPhone/Apple computer) or Alexa will answer your crypto calculations:
"Hey Siri, how much is
1,000 US dollars in Bitcoin?"
Siri: "$1,000 U.S. dollars is
equivalent to 0.30 Bitcoins."

WHERE TO RESEARCH COINS

See the top 100 coins, discover new coins, get quick info, and more at CoinGecko. There's also a mobile app! https://www.coingecko.com

TRACK YOUR CRYPTO FOR TAX PURPOSES

"Under U.S. tax law, Bitcoin and other cryptocurrencies are classified as property and subject to capital gains taxes. But you only owe taxes when those gains are realized." –CNBC

For tax help, visit: https://www.cointracking.info

When the taxman cometh, simply print out all your crypto activity while breathing a sigh of relief.

FOLLOW CRYPTO NEWS

A great, free app called CryptoNews gives you the latest crypto news.

BEST CRYPTO AND STOCK CHARTS

TradingView is excellent. Open a free account here. https://www.tradingview.com/

GET BITCOIN REWARDS FOR SHOPPING ONLINE

Lolli gives you free Bitcoin or cash when you shop at over 1,000 top online stores. https://www.lolli.com

COINBASE LINKS

Join Coinbase: https://www.coinbase.com

CRYPTO TAX GUIDE: https://bit.ly/3zwKXnz

THE PLAN

We save the best for last. Learn the safest and lucrative way to earn crypto: www.ThePlanRocks.com

ABOUT THE AUTHORS

Elaine Wilkes was crypto expert's Dan Hollings first student. She loves researching crypto. She is an internationally published author with Hay House Publishers and a self-published author. Her work has received seven awards. Her latest award-winning book, *War is Personal, Hell, Luck and Resilience*, is her father's raw, honest, and sometimes funny look at life as a combat Marine. She has a Ph.D. in Naturopathy, a Master's Degree in Psychology, and is certified in LEED, Nutrition, and teaching yoga. As an actress, she's appeared in numerous movies, TV shows, and commercials.

Daniel Hall is a *Wall Street Journal* and *USA TODAY* bestselling author, speaker, consultant, coach, lawyer (JD from Texas Tech University), nurse (BSN from University of Texas at El Paso), and host of the popular Daniel Hall YouTube channel. He is also

the creator of the 'Real Fast' brand of training programs designed to help investors, authors, speakers, coaches, consultants, trainers, internet marketers, and entrepreneurs effectively grow their businesses faster and profit more effortlessly.

 **Dan Hollings** is the Internet "Super Strategist," a marketing and E-commerce sought after expert, most well-known for his work with the internationally renowned book/movie, The Secret, and the go-to leader for businesses and manufacturers looking to achieve high levels of success selling on Amazon.

Hollings is now leading the Crypto industry, establishing himself as the guy who cracked the crypto code. Hollings has welcomed thousands through his courses in over 100 countries. His tested and trusted approach removes the hesitation, the fear, and the confusion, and he has a highly proven success rate of helping anyone go from newbie to pro without ever learning how to trade.

From DeFi, to Futures, to Grid Trading, to NFTs as an avid digital art collector and advisor (Desperate ApeWives, CryptoPunks, Board Ape Yacht Club, ArtBlocks and more), Hollings excels in safe strategies with maximum ROI. In addition, he is the creator and teacher of the popular course called "The Plan."

ABOUT THE ILLUSTRATOR

Lisa Rothstein is an illustrator for *The New Yorker Magazine*, bestselling authors and companies in tech and healthcare. Her business, Drawing Out Your Genius™ supports companies in simplifying complex topics, defusing difficult  conversations, and accelerating change through the power of visual communication. She is the co-creator with Daniel Hall of the Real Fast Doodle Profits online training.

Pretty please? If you loved the book, please give it a review on Amazon or wherever you purchased it. That would be awesome sauce!

My Crypto Journal

**No peeking
from anyone else!**

Write in this book!
Or, if you have the digital version,
print two copies of this info and store them in safe
places. Let one trusted person know where they're
located. Investigate about putting this in your will.
Your crypto could become worth a LOT of money.

GENERAL INFO

The unlock code to my phone:	
The unlock code to my computer:	

I cover what I want to be done with my crypto in my will, which is held by:

Name:		
Company:		
Address		
City		
State	Zip	
Phone		
Email		

MY LOGINS AND PASSWORDS FOR SITES I'M USING

Site:	
Username:	
Password:	

Site:	
Username:	
Password:	

Site:	
Username:	
Password:	

Site:	
Username:	
Password:	

Site:	
Username:	
Password:	

Site:	
Username:	
Password:	

Site:	
Username:	
Password:	

Site:	
Username:	
Password:	

Site:	
Username:	
Password:	

Site:	
Username:	
Password:	

Site:	
Username:	
Password:	

Site:	
Username:	
Password:	

IDEAS FOR DIVERSIFYING MY CRYPTO PORTFOLIO

The percentage of my entire portfolio I will use for crypto is: _____

That means I will only use $ _____ for my crypto investments.

IF I dollar cost average my crypto, I will put in: $_____
Circle time frame: Month? Bi-weekly? Other?

I will hold _____ % of my crypto for high- interest savings.

I will take profits with these coins when: _____

_____

I will use these percentages of my crypto portfolio for:

Saving in a high-interest crypto account(s): _____

_____

Trading: _____

_____

Crypto IRAs: _____

_____

Crypto Gridding (from The Plan):_____

_____

CRYPTO IRAs

I have a crypto IRA at:

Site:	
Username:	
Password:	

The person who set up my IRA is: _____

_____

_____

From this company: _____

_____

_____

Phone: _____

Email: _____

MY PURCHASING TRANSACTIONS

Date	Coin	Buying Price	Amount I Invested

MY SELLING TRANSACTIONS

(Check with your financial advisor about the tax
consequences of selling early.)

Date	Coin	Selling Price	Amount I Sold

MY GOALS FOR MY CRYPTO

Writing Down Your Goals Makes Them Happen.

If you enjoyed this book,
you'll love our next crypto book!

This new, easy-peasy book reveals
the secret sauce to earning in crypto.

Go to ez.ht/bonus and sign up to be notified when
it'll be released, so you can get a deal on it.

While you're there, check out our
popular course on safer ways to make higher
earnings in Crypto Land.

Contact us at
1c2cwcbc@gmail.com

Until next time, cheers!

Made in the USA
Coppell, TX
20 January 2022

71996447R00059